AF130774

Stefan Krammer

How to analyze and compare scenarios?

Evaluation of scenarios dealing with the future of our energy system: DESERTEC, EU-Roadmap 2050, Greenpeace [R]evolution, World Energy Outlook & Shell Energy Scenarios

Anchor Compact

Krammer, Stefan: How to analyze and compare scenarios? Evaluation of scenarios dealing with the future of our energy system: DESERTEC, EU-Roadmap 2050, Greenpeace [R]evolution, World Energy Outlook & Shell Energy Scenarios. Hamburg, Anchor Academic Publishing 2013

Original title of the thesis: Characteristics and quality of energy scenarios

Buch-ISBN: 978-3-95489-059-0
PDF-eBook-ISBN: 978-3-95489-559-5
Druck/Herstellung: Anchor Academic Publishing, Hamburg, 2013
Additionally: Karl-Franzens-Universität, Graz, Österreich, Bakkalaureat, 2012

Bibliografische Information der Deutschen Nationalbibliothek:
Die Deutsche Nationalbibliothek verzeichnet diese Publikation in der Deutschen Nationalbibliografie; detaillierte bibliografische Daten sind im Internet über http://dnb.d-nb.de abrufbar

Bibliographical Information of the German National Library:
The German National Library lists this publication in the German National Bibliography. Detailed bibliographic data can be found at: http://dnb.d-nb.de

© Anchor Academic Publishing, ein Imprint der Diplomica® Verlag GmbH
http://www.diplom.de, Hamburg 2013
Printed in Germany

Ehrenwörtliche Erklärung

Ich erkläre ehrenwörtlich, dass ich die vorliegende Arbeit selbstständig und ohne fremde Hilfe verfasst, andere als die angegebenen Quellen nicht benutzt und die den Quellen wörtlich oder inhaltlich entnommenen Stellen als solche kenntlich gemacht habe. Die Arbeit wurde bisher in gleicher oder ähnlicher Form keiner anderen inländischen oder ausländischen Prüfungsbehörde vorgelegt und auch noch nicht veröffentlicht. Die vorliegende Fassung entspricht der eingereichten elektronischen Version.

27. Februar 2012   Unterschrift

Table of Contents

List of figures

List of abbreviations

AC .... Alternate Current

c .... (Euro-)Cent

C .... Celsius

CO_2 .... Carbon dioxide

Comm. .... Communication

CSP .... Concentrated Solar Thermal Power

EU .... European Union

EJ/a .... Exajoule per year

GDP .... Gross Domestic Product

Gt .... Gigaton

HVDC .... High-Voltage Direct Current

IEA .... International Energy Agency

km .... kilometre

kWh .... kilowatt hour

MENA .... Middle East and North Africa

Mtoe .... Million tonnes of oil equivalent

NGO .... Non Governmental Organization

p.a. .... per annum

PJ/a...Petajoule/year

ppm .... parts per million

TWh/a... Terawatt hour/year

1 Introduction

At the moment our energy system is highly dependent on fossil sources, which amount for about 80% of the total primary energy demand with crude oil being the biggest part.[1] This dependency leads to two major problems. Firstly, fossil energy is stored energy from the sun that took millions of years to be developed. Since the long time frames of development, fossil sources are called non-renewable. Since decades pessimists are predicting the end of oil supply, which was postponed in the past because of new discoveries and technological progress. Still crude oil is the scarcest fossil energy source, since the known reserves are enough to last for about 40 years with current depletion. However the current depletion is not enough to supply the increasing energy demand, which is rising by 6,7% p.a., leading to an increase of 50% until 2030. If there are no major changes in the total primary energy demand, it is unavoidable that a lower supply of crude oil will clash with higher demand. A switch to coal seems meaningful since it is the only fossil source that is still abundant. The problem of coal is that it is the dirtiest fossil source in regard to green house gases, which leads directly to the second problem: Climate change. Changes in the climate have occurred ever since in the past, but this time it is the first time that it is caused by residents of the world – human beings. Before the industrial revolution the concentration of carbon dioxide, the chief greenhouse gas that results from human activities and causes global warming amounted 280 ppm, which increased since then to the current amount of 390 ppm.[2] This is the highest concentration of carbon dioxide in the atmosphere in the last 400.000 years of the earth's history. The exact effects of the increased carbon dioxide concentrations on the climate are not known, but there is a scientific consensus that in order to prevent a devastating climate change the emissions have to be dramatically reduced. Since the energy sector is responsible for the bulk of greenhouse gas emissions a switch from oil to coal without technical progress to limit carbon dioxide is not meaningful.[3]

The alternatives to fossil energy sources are on the one hand nuclear energy and on the other hand renewable energy sources. Nuclear energy amounts at the moment for about 5% of the

---

[1]Cf. Quaschning V. (2010): Erneuerbare Energien und Klimaschutz – Hintergründe, Techniken, Anlagenplanung, Wirtschaftlichkeit, Munich, P. 26.
[2]Cf. Forster, P., *et al.* (2007): Changes in Atmospheric Constituents and in Radiative Forcing. in: Solomon, S. *et al.* (eds.)*:* Climate Change 2007: The Physical Science Basis. Contribution of Working Group I to the Fourth Assessment Report of the Intergovernmental Panel on Climate Change, Cambridge and New York, P. 129 -234, P.135.
[3]Cf. McKibben, B. (2009): Our Energy Challenge – Essay by Bill McKibben, in National Geography, Vol.215, Issue 6, P. 1-96, P.24-27.

total primary energy demand. The process of nuclear energy is fascinating, since the energy outcome of one kilogram of uranium equals the stored energy of about 3.000 tons of coal. With an increase of nuclear energy the problem of climate change can be reduced, since the process is carbon neutral. But because of the reason that uranium deposits are also scarce, as well as other problems as, as nuclear proliferation, incidents and the unsolved problem of waste disposal it is be doubted that it will be of great importance in the future.[4]

Renewable energy sources on the other hand have been the major primary energy source before the era of the black gold. Today they amount for about 15% of the total primary energy demand, with biomass and hydro-power having with 10% and 5% the biggest shares. All the other renewable energy sources, as wind power, solar heat and photovoltaic, play a minor role since they don't even cover 1% of the primary energy demand. Renewable energy sources could solve both major problems of the energy sector, since they are carbon neutral and by definition renewable. The drawbacks are that at the moment most renewable sources are not competitive and need to be subsidized by governments and the technical challenge of storing the produced energy.[5]

It is easy to understand that the future of the energy sector is highly uncertain and that tools that are extrapolating past trends are of no use under these circumstances. In the last years several energy scenarios have been conducted, trying to display the major uncertainties. Not surprisingly the results are strongly varying, leading to question of the characteristics and the quality of scenarios. However there has been no analysis of the characteristics and quality of energy scenarios, which is being done in this bachelor thesis.

After a short introduction of the history of scenarios in chapter 2.1, a general framework of the scenario development process is developed in chapter 2.2 and its possible variations are listed in chapter 2.3. The result is a scenario typology consisting of 15 variables that can be used to examine the characteristics and the quality of scenarios. The scenario typology is then applied at a total of 5 scenarios at chapter 2.4. The sample of scenarios was chosen to display the broad range of different scenario developers. It consists of the DESERTEC scenario of a charitable trust, the EU-Roadmap 2050 of a political institution, the Greenpeace [R]evolution of an NGO, the World Energy Outlook of an intergovernmental institution and the Shell Energy scenarios of a company dealing in the energy sector.

---

[4]Cf. Quaschning V. (2010): Erneuerbare Energien und Klimaschutz – Hintergründe, Techniken, Anlagenplanung, Wirtschaftlichkeit, Munich, P. 21-36.
[5]Cf. Quaschning V. (2010): Erneuerbare Energien und Klimaschutz – Hintergründe, Techniken, Anlagenplanung, Wirtschaftlichkeit, Munich, P. 14-35.

2 Scenarios

The last half of the 20th century is characterized by remarkable economic and political coop-
eration caused by increased globalisation. The world population doubled and the world in-
come quadrupled in 50 years. These large increases in the well being of more people are go-
ing hand in hand with more responsibilities, since environmental and resource constraints are
becoming more obvious. For the first time the current generation needs to take into account
the impact for several generations ahead. This background of complex environments, together
with the recent developments of computing power and tools for simulation of large and complex systems are building the basis for the increased interest in scenarios, which are in general
methods in the strategic planning process that are based on the development and analysis of
possible developments in the future.[6]

Figure 1 shows the increase of the peer-reviewed articles on scenarios since 1970.

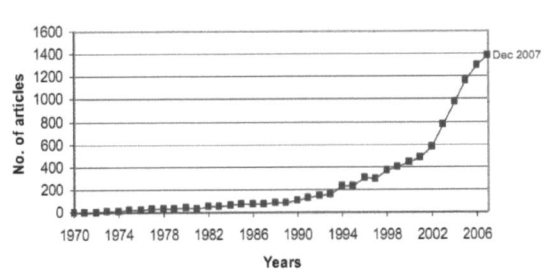

Figure 1: Peer-reviewed articles on scenarios
Source: Ramírez R../ Selsky, J./ Van der Heijden K. (2009): Causal Texture Theories of Turbulence & the
Growth and Role of Scenario Practices, Working Paper, University of Oxford, Liverpool, P.6.

2.1 History

The history of scenarios starts in the 1960s in the field of social psychology and the development of the Casual Texture theory. The theory deals with systems that are trying to survive in
a sustainable way in the outer environment. The system and the environment are connected
with each other, leading to a process of co-evolution, in which the inner system and the outer

---

[6]Cf. Ramírez R./Selsky, J. /Van der Heijden K. (2010a): Preface, in: Ramírez R. (Ed.)/Selsky, J. (Ed.)/Van der
Heijden K. (Ed.): Business Planning for Turbulent Times: New Methods for Applying Scenarios, 2nd ed, London, P. XVI-XX, P.XVI-XVII.

environment systematically influence each other. If there are connections within the outer environment, that the inner system can't influence the contextual environment becomes a source of instability. Under these turbulent circumstances scenarios are helpful for decision makers to understand how the contextual environment may shape in future. This theory influenced the scientific discourse of organisations trying to find strategies fitting to its uncertain business environment.[7]

About the same time, the futurist Hermann Kahn and his colleagues at the RAND Corporation and the Hudson Institute introduced the term scenario planning in the field of social and business sciences.[8] [9] His research was strongly influenced by the cold war, which led to publications of probable, possible and worst-case scenarios of the world, including nuclear war scenarios.[10] Olaf Helmer, who was also employed at the RAND Corporation, focused his scientific work on methodical problems. Together with Norman Dalkey he developed the DELPHI-method, which is still one of the basic tools of futurism.[11]

One of the best known publications of futurism is the book "Limits to Growth", in which the authors analyzed the possible future trends of five variables, which are world population, industrialization, pollution, food production and resource depletion. The main conclusion of the book is that an extrapolation of current trends will lead to fast and unstoppable decline of the world population, food production and industrialization. The reasons for that doomsday are environmental destruction and depletion of natural resources.[12] Although the book was heavily criticized, it is considered to be a pioneer in the field sustainable development and is therefore also of great influence in the energy sector.[13] [14]

The work of futurists and social psychologists influenced the theory and practice of strategy design. Pierre Wack, the former executive of Royal Dutch Shell, is considered among the first to bring these methods and theories to business strategy. He developed multiple, but equally possible scenarios of the future business environment of the company. The use of scenarios

[7]Cf. Ramírez R./Selsky, J./Van der Heijden K. (2010b): Conceptual and Historical Overview, in: Ramírez R. (Ed.)/Selsky, J. (Ed.)/Van der Heijden K. (Ed.): Business Planning for Turbulent Times: New Methods for Applying Scenarios, 2nd ed, London, P.17-30, P.17-18.
[8]Cf. Van der Heijden, K. (2010): Scenarios: The Art of Strategic Conversation, 2.ed., Chichester, P. 3.
[9]Cf. Fink, A. (1999): Szenariogestützte Führung industrieller Produktionsunternehmen, Diss., Paderborn, P. 14-15.
[10]Cf. Kahn H./Wiener A. (1967): The Year 2000 – A Framework for Speculation on the Next Thirty-Three Years, New York, P. 248-358.
[11]Cf. Dalkey, N. (1963): An Experimental Application of the Delphi Method to the Use of Experts, in: Management Science, Vol. 9, Issue 4, P. 458-467, P. 460-467.
[12]Cf. Meadows, D. et al. (1972): Die Grenzen des Wachstums – Bericht des Club of Rome zur Lage der Menschheit, Stuttgart, P. 110-113.
[13]Cf. Rao, P. (2000): Sustainable development: Economics and Policy, Malden, P. 8.
[14]Cf. Rogers, P./Jalal, K./Boyd, J. (2008): An Introduction to Sustainable Development, London, P. 20.

led to a huge advantage at the beginning of the oil crises in 1973 and 1979, since Royal Dutch
Shell had already worked out a suitable strategy in the case of a crisis scenario and was able
to interpret signals for its unfolding correctly, leading to an outperformance of the rest of the
oil industry.[15] Since the success of Royal Dutch Shell, the use of scenario planning as a strategic planning tool is increasing, especially in organisations that are operating in instable
business environments.[16]

The use of scenarios in the field of public planning is still in its infancy, but becoming more
important because of two effects. Firstly, the actions of traditional governance often end up
with unintended side effects.[17] An example in the field of energy policy can be found in
Spain, where the feed-in legislation had the intension to increase the share and technological
progress of renewable energy sources. The unexpected success of the policy led to serious
decreases of coal-fired power generation. Since this clashed with the policy of the protection
of coal-mining employment, the government intervened to protect this industry.[18] Secondly,
the importance of regional integration and globalisation is increasing. This means that many
actions by one national government have an impact above their own boundaries, leading to
more complex environments. Examples are environmental pollution, resource management
and energy policy.[19]

2.2 Scenario Development: A General Framework

A description of a general valid scenario development process is a challenging task, since
scenario planning is considered to be a meta-method, in which different methods contribute to
the content and the quality of the various aspects.[20] This means that no single method of scenario analysis exists, nor can the same method be used in all cases. The structure for creating
scenarios has to be flexible to fit to its various purposes.[21]

---

[15]Cf. Van der Heijden, K. (2010): Scenarios: The Art of Strategic Conversation, 2.ed., Chichester, P. 3-10.
[16]Cf. Fink, A. (1999): Szenariogestützte Führung industrieller Produktionsunternehmen, Diss., Paderborn, P. 16.
[17]Cf. Arvidsson N. (2010): Designing More Effective Political Governance of Turbulent Fields: The Case of
Health Care, in: Ramírez R. (Ed.)/Selsky, J. (Ed.)/Van der Heijden K. (Ed.): Business Planning for Turbulent
Times: New Methods for Applying Scenarios, 2nd ed, London, P.131 -146, P.133-134.
[18]Cf. BP (ed.) (2011): BP Statistical Review of World Energy June 2011, http://bp.com/statisticalreview, October 5th 2011.
[19]Cf. Arvidsson N. (2010): Designing More Effective Political Governance of Turbulent Fields: The Case of
Health Care, in: Ramírez R. (Ed.)/Selsky, J. (Ed.)/Van der Heijden K. (Ed.): Business Planning for Turbulent
Times: New Methods for Applying Scenarios, 2nd ed, London, P.131 -146, P.133-134.
[20]Cf. Fink, A. (1999): Szenariogestützte Führung industrieller Produktionsunternehmen, Diss., Paderborn, P. 96.
[21]Cf. Masini, E/Vasques J. (2000): Scenarios as Seen from a Human and Social Perspective, in: Technological
Forecasting and Social Change, Vol. 5, Issue 1, P. 49-66, P.66.

However, given the observed diversity of scenarios, one can only analyze and compare scenarios in a credible and consistent manner when there is a shared understanding of the commonalties of the scenario development process.[22] Figure 2 shows the general framework of the scenario development process, which will be described in detail in this chapter. Deviations from the general framework and variations within the framework will be presented in chapter 2.3. Both the general framework and the deviations and variations are essential for the analysis of different energy scenarios.

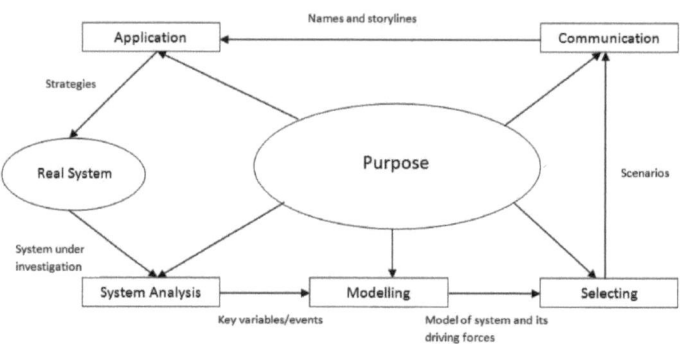

Figure 2: The general framework of the Scenario Development Process
Source: Cf. Zürni, S. (2004): Möglichkeiten und Grenzen der Szenarioanalyse – Eine Analyse am Beispiel der Schweizer Energieplanung, Stuttgart and Berlin, P. 223.

2.2.1 Purpose

The starting point of every scenario development process is the definition of the purpose of the analysis. Furthermore the methods, the time frame and the system boundaries of the system under investigation have to be determined.[23]

The purpose is of great importance since it influences all the other stages of the general framework, meaning that an unclear purpose will lead to poor results.[24]

2.2.2 System Analysis

In this step the real existing system and its properties are examined. The most challenging part is to gain accurate data that effect the future development of the system. Not surprisingly, this

---

[22]Cf. Van Notten, P. *et al.* (2003): An updated scenario typology, in Futures, Vol.35, Issue 5, P. 423-443, P.423.
[23]Cf. Zürni, S. (2004): Möglichkeiten und Grenzen der Szenarioanalyse – Eine Analyse am Beispiel der Schweizer Energieplanung, Stuttgart and Berlin, P. 224.
[24]Cf. Lindgren, M./Brandhold, H. (2009): Scenario Planning : The Link between Future and Strategy, rev. and updated ed., Basingstoke, P. 56.

step is exposed to large number of possible variations, depending on the defined purpose, as well as the availability and form of data. Nevertheless a general procedure can be described.[25]

In order to identify and collect data, which is at least relevant for the defined purpose, the scenario developer has to choose between a broad variety of methods. The integration of experts via interviews or workshops is most commonly used. The gathered data is then divided into two classes. Firstly internal data, which has the characteristic, that the scenario user has an impact on the future development of it. Secondly external data, that can't be influenced by the scenario user. In this stage the focus is on the external data, which is of the form that it is representing the external environment of the system. The next step is to evaluate what parts of the external environment are predictable and which are uncertain. Predetermines, where there are no different interpretations of what is happening and therefore not exposed to uncertainty are to be neglected in this stage, but included in the process later as described in chapter 2.2.5. In this stage, the attention is on external data that is uncertain, meaning that it is impossible to exactly describe the future outcome or even the existing state with certainty. Because of simplification it is usual that the uncertainties are reduced to those factors with the largest effect on the purpose.[26]

2.2.3 Modelling

The aim of this step is to model the events, patterns, trends and of most importance the underlying structure of the system under investigation, which are illustrated in the "System Thinking Iceberg Model" in Figure 3. The upper part of the iceberg is the event level, which is visible and can be observed. It is the level that describes how human beings perceive and describe the world. An example in the field of energy is the availability of energy at any time on demand.

The second level of the iceberg model is the level of patterns and trends, which are changes in the events that occur over time. For an examination of patterns the relationships between various events have to be found and described. As shown in Figure 3 this level is under water, metaphorically meaning that it is challenging but possible to see the patterns and trends. An example of a trend in the field of energy is the increase in the oil price since the millennium change.

---

[25]Cf. Zürni, S. (2004): Möglichkeiten und Grenzen der Szenarioanalyse – Eine Analyse am Beispiel der Schweizer Energieplanung, Stuttgart and Berlin, P. 224.
[26]Cf. Van der Heijden, K. (2010): Scenarios: The Art of Strategic Conversation, 2.ed., Chichester, P. 228-230.

The last level is the structure. The structure supports and creates the patterns and trends, which are leading to events that can easily be seen. Structures are composed by the relationship of patterns and trends. The description of structure is difficult, because as metaphorically shown in Figure 3, it is impossible to see it.[27]

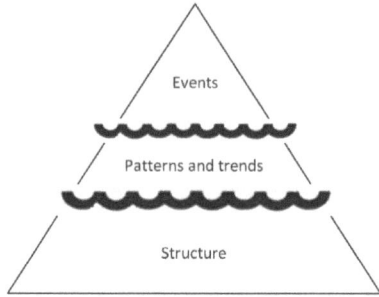

Figure 3: System Thinking Iceberg Model
Source: Cf. Senge, P. (1992): The Fifth Discipline. The Art and Practice of the Learning Organization, London, P. 93-114.

The data that was collected in the step of the System analysis represents the visible part of the iceberg metaphor. In order to derive the patterns and trends as well as the underlying structure of the system the scenario developer has to start with finding logic clusters about the uncertain environmental factors. Those clusters are then modelled and studied in depth in order to derive the driving forces that are the main reason of the trends and patterns.[28]

In the praxis of the scenario development process, it is usual to start with the most important key events and develop simple causal loop diagrams, which visualise how the variables are affecting one another. The relationships are represented by arrows that are labelled positive or negative. A positive label means that an increase of the variable leads to an increase of the dependent variable, whereas a negative label means that an increase of the variable leads to a decrease of the dependent one. The main task is to identify driving forces, which are the main reason for the changes in the future behaviour of the environment and which are interdepend-

[27]Cf. Senge, P. (1992): The Fifth Discipline. The Art & Practice of The Learning Organization, London, P. 93-114.
[28]Cf. Van der Heijden, K. (2010): Scenarios: The Art of Strategic Conversation, 2.ed., Chichester, P. 230.

ent of other examined variables. The modelling process is finished when the model sufficiently represents the underlying structure of the system.[29]

Figure 4 represents a simple causal loop diagram, where the price of renewable energy is the key event and the price of fossil energy and governmental funding are regarded to be the two main driving forces.

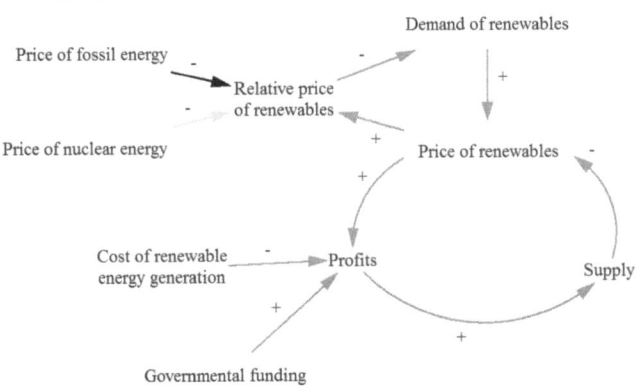

Figure 4: CLD representing the underlying structure of the price of renewable energy
Source: Own illustration

As a final step theories about the future behaviour of the driving forces have to be conducted. Since the driving forces have a big impact on the event level through causal links it is then possible to examine plausible developments of the visible part of the system.[30]

2.2.4 Selecting

Scenarios are formed through combination of possible future behaviours of the various driving forces. Because many combinations can be meaningful, the problem of selecting the most suitable ones occurs.[31] The usual number of selected scenarios is between two and four, since

[29]Cf. Van der Heijden, K. (2010): Scenarios: The Art of Strategic Conversation, 2.ed., Chichester, P. 230- 235.
[30]Cf. Zürni, S. (2004): Möglichkeiten und Grenzen der Szenarioanalyse – Eine Analyse am Beispiel der Schweizer Energieplanung, Stuttgart and Berlin, P. 225.
[31]Cf. Zürni, S. (2004): Möglichkeiten und Grenzen der Szenarioanalyse – Eine Analyse am Beispiel der Schweizer Energieplanung, Stuttgart and Berlin, P. 225.

more than four scenarios are proven to be organisationally impractical and only one cannot reflect uncertainty.[32]

Again there is not the one-fits-all method of selecting scenarios, but all methods are based on the following requirements of the chosen ones:[33] [34] [35]

- Consistency: The cause-effect chains of the scenarios are internally consistent.
- Plausibility: The scenarios are realistically plausible.
- Relevance: The scenarios lead to useful insights of the defined purpose.
- Differentiation: The scenarios are structurally or qualitatively different.
- Challenging: The scenario challenges mental models and leads to new and original perspectives.

2.2.5 Communication

In this step the chosen scenarios are communicated to a more or less broad public. The communication process consists of two steps. Firstly, each scenario is to be named. Most authors argue in favour for a short memorable descriptive title, that is eliciting a rich imagery. Secondly a storyline has to be developed, which links the past, present and the possible future in a narrative way. The different interpretations of the driving forces are transparently worked out, whereas the predetermines are reflected in each storyline, as shown in Figure 5.[36] [37]

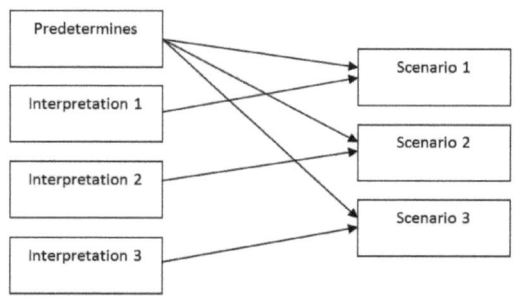

Figure 5: Relationship of predetermines and interpretations in scenarios
Source: Cf. Van der Heijden K. (2010): Scenarios: The Art of Strategic Conversation, 2.ed., Chichester, P. 92.

[32]Cf. Van der Heijden, K. (2010): Scenarios: The Art of Strategic Conversation, 2.ed., Chichester, P. 225.
[33]Cf. Zürni, S. (2004): Möglichkeiten und Grenzen der Szenarioanalyse – Eine Analyse am Beispiel der Schweizer Energieplanung, Stuttgart and Berlin, P. 225.
[34]Cf. Lindgren, M./Brandhold, H. (2009): Scenario Planning : The Link between Future and Strategy, rev. and updated ed., Basingstoke, P. 33-34.
[35]Cf. Van der Heijden, K. (2010): Scenarios: The Art of Strategic Conversation, 2.ed., Chichester, P.225-226.
[36]Cf. Van der Heijden, K. (2010): Scenarios: The Art of Strategic Conversation, 2.ed., Chichester, P. 259-261.
[37]Cf. Lindgren, M./Brandhold, H. (2009): Scenario Planning : The Link between Future and Strategy, rev. and updated ed., Basingstoke, P. 74-82.

2.2.6 Application

The application of scenarios is the link between insights and action. The output of the previous steps as such is not leading to concrete action, but the understanding of the underlying structure and its driving forces are usually leading to opportunities of leverage that have been unknown before. The scenario user is therefore searching for suitable actions in the case of the unfolding of the communicated scenarios.[38]

This stage is again exposed to a large number of possible variations, depending on the defined purpose and the possible influence of the scenario user on the system. It is even possible, that scenarios are solely conducted for a learning process and that there is no implicit application at all. Nevertheless in this paper it is assumed that those scenarios could be applied by third parties.

2.3 Characteristics of Scenarios

As already mentioned in chapter 2.2 there exists no one-fits-all method of scenario analysis, nor can the same method be used in all cases. The structure for creating scenarios has to be flexible to fit to its various purposes.[39]

In order to improve the analysis and the comparison of differently developed scenarios a scenario typology is described in the following chapter, representing all deviations from the general framework and variations within it. There have been many descriptions of typologies in the scientific literature of scenarios. However, older studies[40][41] have focused on characteristics of a specific field, as an industry sector. Unsurprisingly there have been huge differences in the proposed typologies. The biggest drawback of those typologies is that it is impossible to compare scenarios from different fields. In contrast to the older ones, are newer studies[42][43][44] aiming to capture the diversity of scenarios to be able to integrate the broad varieties in the

---

[38]Cf. Van der Heijden, K. (2010): Scenarios: The Art of Strategic Conversation, 2.ed., Chichester, P.273.
[39]Cf. Masini, E/Vasques J. (2000): Scenarios as Seen from a Human and Social Perspective, in: Technological Forecasting and Social Change, Vol. 5, Issue 1, P. 49-66, P.66.
[40]Cf. Gobet M./Rubelat F.(1996): The Use and Misuse of Scenarios, in: Long Range Planning, Vol. 29, Issue 2, P. 164-171, P.166-170.
[41]Cf. Heugens P./Van Oosterhout J. (2001): To boldly go where no man has gone before: integrating cognitive and physical features in scenario studies, in Futures, Vol. 33, Issue 10, P. 861-872, P. 862-871.
[42]Cf. Van Notten, P. *et al.* (2003): An updated scenario typology, in Futures, Vol.35, Issue 5, P. 423-443, P.423-434.
[43]Cf. Zürni, S. (2004): Möglichkeiten und Grenzen der Szenarioanalyse – Eine Analyse am Beispiel der Schweizer Energieplanung, Stuttgart and Berlin, P. 243-256.
[44]Cf. Fink, A. (1999): Szenariogestützte Führung industrieller Produktionsunternehmen, Diss., Paderborn, P. 29-45.

scenario development process in the typology. Those studies led to similar results, although they have been conducted independently from each other.

2.3.1 Variations in Purpose

In this chapter variations in the purpose of the scenario are presented. Since the purpose has effects on all the other stages, variations presented in these chapters also influence all the following steps of the scenario development process.

2.3.1.1 Time Scale

Depending on the temporal or time scale, scenarios are classified in long-term and short-term scenarios:[45][46][47]

- Long term scenarios are having time horizons until far in the future. Scenarios that have time scales of 25 years or more are classified as long termed.

- Short term scenarios have a shorter time horizon than 25 years, usually about 3 to 10 years. Short term scenarios are especially useful in fields that are characterized by highly complex and uncertain system, as for example the growth of GDP.

2.3.1.2 Vantage Point

Depending on the vantage point and the inclusion of norms and values, scenarios are classified in normative and explorative scenarios:[48][49][50]

- Normative scenarios have consciously included norms and values. Normative scenarios start with the description of preferable and desirable future situation and are scrutinizing what developments are needed in order for them to occur. Since normative scenarios are starting from the future this approach is often referred as backcasting.

---

[45]Cf. Van Notten, P. *et al.* (2003): An updated scenario typology, in Futures, Vol.35, Issue 5, P. 423-443, P.430-431.
[46]Cf. Fink, A. (1999): Szenariogestützte Führung industrieller Produktionsunternehmen, Diss., Paderborn, P. 34-39.
[47]Cf. Zürni, S. (2004): Möglichkeiten und Grenzen der Szenarioanalyse – Eine Analyse am Beispiel der Schweizer Energieplanung, Stuttgart and Berlin, P. 247.
[48]Cf. Van Notten, P. *et al.* (2003): An updated scenario typology, in Futures, Vol.35, Issue 5, P. 423-443, P.429..
[49]Cf. Fink, A. (1999): Szenariogestützte Führung industrieller Produktionsunternehmen, Diss., Paderborn, P. 34-39.
[50]Cf. Zürni, S. (2004): Möglichkeiten und Grenzen der Szenarioanalyse – Eine Analyse am Beispiel der Schweizer Energieplanung, Stuttgart and Berlin, P. 248.

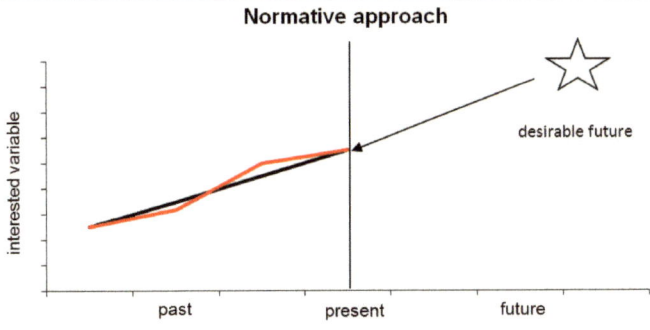

Figure 6: The normative approach
Source: Own illustration

- Explorative or descriptive scenarios do not consciously include norms and values. Starting from the present situation and the analysis of the development of driving forces future situations are described, independent of their desirability. These scenarios usually refer to possible or probable scenarios. Since even explorative scenarios are unable to perfectly exclude values and interests of the scenario development team they cannot be regarded as value-free.

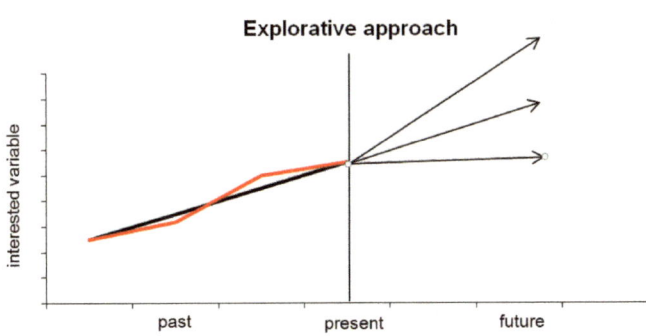

Figure 7: The explorative approach
Source: Own Illustration

2.3.1.3 Subject

Scenarios also differ according the subject of the purpose, where a classification in issue-based, area based and institution-based scenarios is meaningful. Overlaps between the three categories are possible:[51]

- Issue-based scenarios have a defined issue or topic of the study, as for example the future of energy.
- Area based scenarios describe possible futures of a particular geographical area, such as a country or a city.
- Institution based scenarios are based on the future development of the environment of an institution, as a company.

2.3.1.4 Temporal nature

The temporal nature, which distinguishes between process and situation scenarios, should not be confused with the time scale:[52] [53] [54]

- Process scenarios include the descriptions of pathways that are leading from the current situation to a certain future situation.
- Situation scenarios focus on the description of the future situations, thereby neglecting or only implicitly addressing the pathway that result in the end-state. Situation scenarios are a deviation from the general framework and it has to be scrutinized if the description of the future state is a scenario or rather a vision.

2.3.1.5 Spatial scales

The spatial scale of scenarios ranges from the global level to supranational areas, down to national and regional areas. A simplification is to use only the following two categories:[55]

- Global and Supranational scenarios take into considerations big spatial levels as the whole world and supranational entities, as the European Union.
- National and local scenarios focus on a smaller spatial level, as countries, areas and regions.

---

[51]Cf. Van Notten, P. *et al.* (2003): An updated scenario typology, in Futures, Vol.35, Issue 5, P. 423-443, P.429.
[52]Cf. Van Notten, P. *et al.* (2003): An updated scenario typology, in Futures, Vol.35, Issue 5, P. 423-443, P.433.
[53]Cf. Fink, A. (1999): Szenariogestützte Führung industrieller Produktionsunternehmen, Diss., Paderborn, P. 39-45.
[54]Cf. Zürni, S. (2004): Möglichkeiten und Grenzen der Szenarioanalyse – Eine Analyse am Beispiel der Schweizer Energieplanung, Stuttgart and Berlin, P. 248.
[55]Cf. Van Notten, P. *et al.* (2003): An updated scenario typology, in Futures, Vol.35, Issue 5, P. 423-443, P.431.

2.3.2 Variations in System Analysis

The system analysis, where data is collected that is representing the real existing system mainly differs in the way how data is collected and according the nature of the data.

2.3.2.1 Method of data collection

The data and information needed for scenarios can be collected in the following two ways:[56] [57]

- Desk research means that the data is collected without any participatory process. This includes amongst other methods the collection and analysis of data through scientific journals and computer simulations.

- The participatory approach uses certain processes between individuals for the gathering of information. This approach might draw on experts in the field, decision-makers and all kind of stakeholders. There are various organisational structures of participatory processes as workshops and Future Conferences.

2.3.2.2 Nature of data

Depending on the nature of data scenarios can be characterised as qualitative or quantitative scenarios. Since overlaps of both are possible and common in the scenario development process the third category, which is including both qualitative and quantitative is meaningful:[58] [59] [60]

- Qualitative Scenarios are dealing with data that is nominal or ordinal scaled. Ordinal scaled means that the different values of the data cannot be compared or be put in any order. Ordinal scaled data have the characteristics that the values are of different intensity and can be put in order.[61] The use of qualitative data is appropriate if the analysed system is of high complexity and when the information cannot be quantified. In

---

[56]Cf. Van Notten, P. *et al.* (2003): An updated scenario typology, in Futures, Vol.35, Issue 5, P. 423-443, P.432.
[57]Cf. Fink, A. (1999): Szenariogestützte Führung industrieller Produktionsunternehmen, Diss., Paderborn, P. 39-45.
[58]Cf. Van Notten, P. *et al.* (2003): An updated scenario typology, in Futures, Vol.35, Issue 5, P. 423-443, P.431-432.
[59]Cf. Fink, A. (1999): Szenariogestützte Führung industrieller Produktionsunternehmen, Diss., Paderborn, P. 31-34.
[60]Cf. Zürni, S. (2004): Möglichkeiten und Grenzen der Szenarioanalyse – Eine Analyse am Beispiel der Schweizer Energieplanung, Stuttgart and Berlin, P. 249-250.
[61]Cf. Hartung J./Elpelt B./Klösener K. (2005): Statistik – Lehr und Handbuch der angewandten Statistik, 14.ed., München, P. 16-17.

the absence of quantitative data the scenario process usually relies on soft methods as the judgement and intuition of persons.[62]

- Quantitative Scenarios are dealing with data that are interval or ratio scaled. In interval scaled data the values can be put in an order and the distance between the values can be interpreted meaningfully. In addition to that ratio scaled data have an absolute zero.[63] With the availability of quantitative data, the use of mathematical tools and computer models is meaningful.[64]

- Scenarios with both qualitative and quantitative data are using data on all scale measurements in order to make the scenario analysis more consistent and robust. The drawback of this approach is that the fusion of qualitative and quantitative data is a methodical challenge.

2.3.3 Variations in Modelling

The step of modelling, where the underlying structure of the system is modelled and the driving forces for future developments are derived mainly differs according the number of driving forces and the nature of dynamics.

2.3.3.1 Number of driving forces

This characteristic addresses the number of examined driving forces in the scenario development process and is an indicator for the complexity and uncertainty of the model.[65]

- Small amount refers to scenarios with less than 10 examined driving forces, in the model building.

- Medium amount means that in the scenario analysis 10 to 20 driving forces have been examined. A reduction of the driving forces is meaningful.

- Large amount addresses to scenarios that are using more than 20 driving forces in the modelling process. Because of the resulting complexity a reduction of the driving forces is usually conducted.

---

[62]Cf. Fink, A. (1999): Szenariogestützte Führung industrieller Produktionsunternehmen, Diss., Paderborn, P. 34-39.
[63]Cf. Hartung J./Elpelt B./Klösener K. (2005): Statistik – Lehr und Handbuch der angewandten Statistik, 14.ed., München, P. 17.
[64]Cf. Fink, A. (1999): Szenariogestützte Führung industrieller Produktionsunternehmen, Diss., Paderborn, P. 34-39.
[65]Cf. Zürni, S. (2004): Möglichkeiten und Grenzen der Szenarioanalyse – Eine Analyse am Beispiel der Schweizer Energieplanung, Stuttgart and Berlin, P. 250.

2.3.3.2 The nature of the dynamics

Depending on the nature of dynamics scenarios are distinguished in peripheral and surprise-free trend scenarios:[66] [67] [68]

- Peripheral scenarios, which are often also called extreme or contrast scenarios describe a discontinuous pathway to the future, including unlikely and extreme trends. Those scenarios describe possible situations in which there is only a short period of time of leverage that requires decisive actions.
- Trend scenarios are probable pathways to the futures, extrapolating from existing trends. Trend scenarios have to be scrutinized if the analysis is a scenario or rather a forecast. Usually trend scenarios are building the basis of peripheral scenarios, in order to show the deviation from the trend and the extreme outcome.

2.3.4 Variations in Selecting

In the selecting process possible future behaviours of driving forces are combined to scenarios according to some basic requirements. The most important variation in this step is if the selection is done in an inductive, deductive or incremental way.

2.3.4.1 Scenario building approach

The most important characteristic in the selecting process is the decision if it is being done by using an inductive, deductive or an incremental approach.[69] [70] [71]

- Inductive scenarios are characterized by a reasoning that makes generalizations based on individual factors. The possible future behaviours of the driving forces come first and the logic follows later. The individual future states of the driving forces are combined into a logic and consistent order, which usually requires several iterations until satisfactory scenarios are developed. It is of great importance that the inductive scenarios do not end up in having a normative statement, meaning that one scenario is more preferred than the other.

---

[66]Cf. Van Notten, P. *et al.* (2003): An updated scenario typology, in Futures, Vol.35, Issue 5, P. 423-443, P.433.
[67]Cf. Fink, A. (1999): Szenariogestützte Führung industrieller Produktionsunternehmen, Diss., Paderborn, P. 31-34.
[68]Cf. Zürni, S. (2004): Möglichkeiten und Grenzen der Szenarioanalyse – Eine Analyse am Beispiel der Schweizer Energieplanung, Stuttgart and Berlin, P. 248.
[69]Cf. Van der Heijden, K. (2010): Scenarios: The Art of Strategic Conversation, 2.ed., Chichester, P. 236-254.
[70]Cf. Fink, A. (1999): Szenariogestützte Führung industrieller Produktionsunternehmen, Diss., Paderborn, P. 34-39.
[71]Cf. Zürni, S. (2004): Möglichkeiten und Grenzen der Szenarioanalyse – Eine Analyse am Beispiel der Schweizer Energieplanung, Stuttgart and Berlin, P. 247.

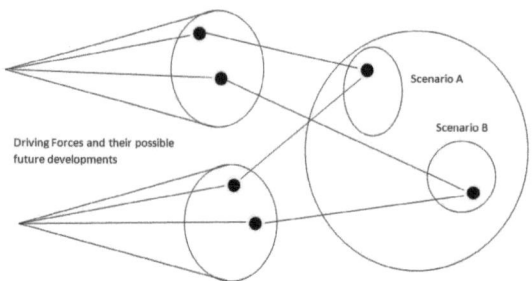

Figure 8: Inductive Scenario Building Approach
Source: Cf. Fink, A. (1999): Szenariogestützte Führung industrieller Produktionsunternehmen, Diss., Paderborn, P. 97.

- Deductive scenarios are characterized by a reasoning that a conclusion logically and necessarily follows from a certain set of premises. In the praxis of scenario development a framework or an overall structure is used to delimit the scenario building process. The uncertain driving forces are reduced to the two or three most important ones and for each driving force two possible future outcomes are constructed. Through a combination of the possible future developments of the two critical driving forces a matrix of four scenarios, or in the case of three driving forces a cube of nine scenarios is described.

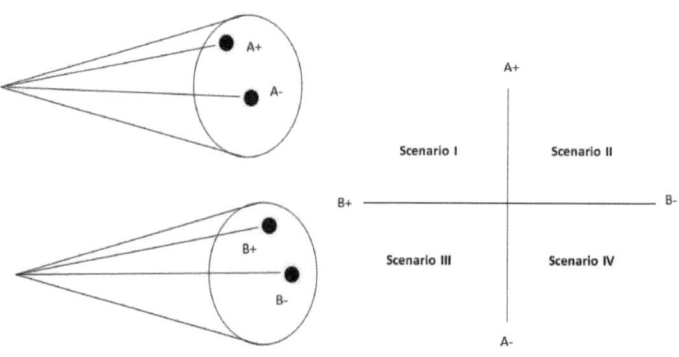

Figure 9: Deductive Scenario Building Approach
Source: Cf. Fink, A. (1999): Szenariogestützte Führung industrieller Produktionsunternehmen, Diss., Paderborn, P. 100.

20

- Incremental scenarios are using as a basis the extrapolation of existing trends, which are leading to the most probable trend scenario. By using a kind of sensitivity analysis of the driving forces various scenarios are being developed.

2.3.4.2 Level of deviation

The level of deviation refers to the range of possible futures that are taken in account:[72] [73]

- Focused scenarios focus on a very small area of all the possible futures, usually only on one single scenario. Again it has to be scrutinized if the description of the future state is a scenario or a pure forecast, which is extrapolating past trends. The advantages of focused scenarios are that all the resources can be concentrated to one scenario and a simplified communication. However the focus on only one scenario is regarded to contradict the initial purpose of scenarios, of being a method able to deal with a high level of uncertainty.

- Planning focused scenarios deal with multiple scenarios, but focussing on a certain area. These scenarios are usually the starting point of strategy development.

- Alternative scenarios try to map all possible futures. Hence the scenarios are differing significantly from each other. These scenarios are usually developed to raise awareness of the uncertainties and to experiment with varying ideas.

2.3.4.3 Estimation of probability

Depending if the different key variables can be attached with certain probabilities the scenarios can the distinguished in prognoses and projections.[74] [75]

- Prognosis scenarios are attached with at least a subjective probability of occurrence. They are a deviation of the general framework and are contradicting most definitions of scenarios. Therefore it has to be scrutinized if the prognosis scenario is a scenario or rather a forecast.

---

[72]Cf. Van Notten, P. *et al.* (2003): An updated scenario typology, in Futures, Vol.35, Issue 5, P. 423-443, P.433-434.
[73]Cf. Fink, A. (1999): Szenariogestützte Führung industrieller Produktionsunternehmen, Diss., Paderborn, P. 31-34.
[74]Cf. Fink, A. (1999): Szenariogestützte Führung industrieller Produktionsunternehmen, Diss., Paderborn, P. 31-34.
[75]Cf. Zürni, S. (2004): Möglichkeiten und Grenzen der Szenarioanalyse – Eine Analyse am Beispiel der Schweizer Energieplanung, Stuttgart and Berlin, P. 248.

- Projections do not include any calculus of probabilities. The absence of probabilities is justified because of its low informational value, especially at complex underlying systems and because of methodical challenges.

-

2.3.5 Variations in Communication

The communication of scenarios varies according the effort that is put in the flow of information of the published scenarios.

2.3.5.1 Effort of communication

Depending on the effort of communication, low effort, medium effort and high effort communication can be distinguished:[76] [77] [78]

- Low effort communication is characterized solely by the usage of a memorable title for the scenario. There is no description of the storyline from the present to the possible future state. Since most definitions of scenarios also include the trajectory line to the possible future state it can be doubted if these are high-quality scenarios.
- Medium-effort communication is developing next to the title also a storyline, which is a narrative link of the past with hypothetical events in the future. Hence it is a description of a possible path of to the future. The storyline has to be transparent and internally consistent. Predetermined elements have to be reflected in each storyline.
- High-effort communication is developing next to the storyline further tools, as diagrams describing the differences of the scenarios, a list of the quantified key variables and indicators, a System Dynamics Approach to quantify the storyline and validations and judgements by experts.

-

2.3.6 Variations in Application

The application of scenarios is leading to concrete actions according to the goals of the scenario user.

---

[76]Cf. Van der Heijden, K. (2010): Scenarios: The Art of Strategic Conversation, 2.ed., Chichester, P. 260-261.
[77]Cf. Lindgren, M./Brandhold, H. (2009): Scenario Planning : The Link between Future and Strategy, rev. and updated ed., Basingstoke, P. 74-82.
[78]Cf. Zürni, S. (2004): Möglichkeiten und Grenzen der Szenarioanalyse – Eine Analyse am Beispiel der Schweizer Energieplanung, Stuttgart and Berlin, P. 252-253.

2.3.6.1 Preciseness of problem

Decisions which are justified by scenarios can rely on precise or on intuitive problems. Depending on the preciseness of the problem scenarios can be used either as decision and orientation projects:[79] [80]

- Decision projects are using scenarios for the justification for the use of a certain action out of a set of already existing alternatives, which optimally suits the achievement of objectives. These scenarios have a direct effect on the formation of the organisational decisions.
- Orientation projects on the other hand lead to a specification of general decision behaviours. These scenarios have a direct effect on the formation of mission statements, strategies and the development of action alternatives.

2.3.6.2 Manoeuvrability

The manoeuvrability is an important criterion for the choice of the scenario field. The characteristic manoeuvrability can be divided in the following 3 dimensions:[81] [82]

- Environmental scenarios solely deal with developments of uncertainties on which the scenario user has no impact. Hence there is no manoeuvrability given in these scenarios.
- Areas of influence scenarios solely deal with developments of internal uncertainties on which the user has an impact. The scenario user can choose between the alternative scenarios. Area of system scenarios are a deviation of the general framework and are highly criticised by experts, because they are not dealing with any kind of unrulable uncertainty.[83]
- System scenarios include both internal manoeuvrable uncertainties and external uncertainties. Hence the system user has a limited manoeuvrability.

---

[79]Cf. Fink, A. (1999): Szenariogestützte Führung industrieller Produktionsunternehmen, Diss., Paderborn, P. 39-45.
[80]Cf. Zürni, S. (2004): Möglichkeiten und Grenzen der Szenarioanalyse – Eine Analyse am Beispiel der Schweizer Energieplanung, Stuttgart and Berlin, P. 247.
[81]Cf. Fink, A. (1999): Szenariogestützte Führung industrieller Produktionsunternehmen, Diss., Paderborn, P. 39-45.
[82]Cf. Zürni, S. (2004): Möglichkeiten und Grenzen der Szenarioanalyse – Eine Analyse am Beispiel der Schweizer Energieplanung, Stuttgart and Berlin, P. 247.
[83]Cf. Schnaars, S. (1987): How to Develop and Use Scenarios, in: Long Range Planning, Vol. 20, Issue 1, P. 105-114, P.112.

2.3.7 Scenario typology

Figure 10 represents a complete table of the variations presented in this chapter and can be used as a checklist for the comparisons and analysis of various scenarios.

Level	Characteristic	Possible Variations		
Purpose	Time Scale	Long Term		Short Term
	Vantage Point	Normative		Explorative
	Subject	Issue	Area	Institution
	Temporal Nature	Process		Situation
	Spatial Scale	Global/Supranational		National/Regional
System Analysis	Data Collection	Desk Research		Participatory Approach
	Nature of Data	Qualitative	Quantitative	Both types
Modelling	Driving Forces	Small (>10)	Medium (10-20)	Large (<20)
	Nature of Dynamics	Peripheral		Trend
Selecting	Scenario Building	Inductive	Deductive	Incremental
	Deviation	Focused	Planning Focused	Alternative
	Probability Estimation	Prognosis		Projection
Comm.	Effort	Low	Medium	High
Application	Preciseness of Problem	Decision		Orientation
	Manoeuvrability	Environmental	Area of Influence	System Scenario

Figure 10: The Scenario Typology
Source: Cf. Fink, A. (1999): Szenariogestützte Führung industrieller Produktionsunternehmen, Diss., Paderborn, P. 45. Cf. Zürni, S. (2004): Möglichkeiten und Grenzen der Szenarioanalyse – Eine Analyse am Beispiel der Schweizer Energieplanung, Stuttgart and Berlin, P. 244-246. Cf. Van Notten, P. et al. (2003): An updated scenario typology, in Futures, Vol.35, Issue 5, P. 423-443, P.426.

2.4 Energy Scenarios

In this chapter a sample of five energy scenarios are summarized, mainly focusing on the development of the total energy demand with its various energy efficiency potentials as well as the future energy mix. Furthermore the methodical and analytical aspects of the various scenarios are scrutinized according the scenario typology that was presented in Figure 10.

2.4.1 DESERTEC

DESERTEC is a concept for the production of renewable energy, with a strong focus on concentrated solar power (CSP) in the Sahara desert, which is transported over far distances to the centres of demand in Europe and MENA.

The DESERTEC concept has its roots in two symposia organized by the club of Rome in 2003, where the switch to renewable energy sources has been regarded as the solution for the climate challenge. In order to achieve this energy shift a masterplan for climate and energy security was devised, that has its scientific roots on two studies[84] [85] that were conducted by the German Federal Ministry for the Environment, Nature Conservation and Nuclear Safety.[86]

The scenario examines two driving forces of the future electricity consumption, which are population and economic growth. Population growth is expected to stabilize in both Europe and MENA at about 600 million inhabitants until 2050, whereas the economic growth is expected to continue its past trend. Given that numbers the electricity consumption in 2050 is assumed to be about 3.000 TWh/a in MENA and 4.000 TWh/a in Europe. A description of needed energy efficiency measures, leading to the final demand is not part of the scenario.

Based on this future electricity consumption a portfolio of renewable energy sources is built that is able to cover both the peak and base-load demand in the future. A big emphasis is put on CSP, since it has with a technical electricity potential of 630.000 TWh/a by far the best potential of all renewable sources. Furthermore it is able to deliver base-load power through sunshine during the day and by the use of thermal energy storage facilities during night. As shown in Figure 11 the scenario is characterized by a boom of renewable energy sources after the year 2020 and a phasing out of nuclear energy as well as a stagnation of fossil sources, which will be used only as a backup. A substantial amount of solar energy is exported from MENA to Europe, which requires High-Voltage Direct Current (HVDC) interconnections between the areas of Scandinavia to the Sahara. Since their minimal transmission losses of 10-15% over a distance of 3000 km the HVDC transmission will have the function of energy highways, whereas the conventional alternate current (AC) grid will deliver the energy to the

---

[84]Cf. Trieb, F. *et al.* (2006): TRANS-CSP - Trans-Mediterranean Interconnection for Concentrating Solar Power. Final Report, http://www.dlr.de/tt/trans-csp, January 12th 2012, P. 1-190.
[85]Cf. Trieb, F. *et al.* (2005): MED-CSP – Concentrating Solar Power for the Mediterranean Region. Final Report, http://www.dlr.de/tt/med-csp, January 12th 2012, P. 1-285.
[86]Cf. Knies, G. (2011): TREC und DESERTEC: Die Entstehung des Konzepts, in: The Club of Rome (ed.): Der DESERTEC Atlas – Weltatlas zu den erneuerbaren Energien, Hamburg, P.114-117, P. 114-116.

consumers at low-voltage levels. Based on estimated future solar electricity costs of 5c per kWh Europe will import 15% of its energy demand.[87]

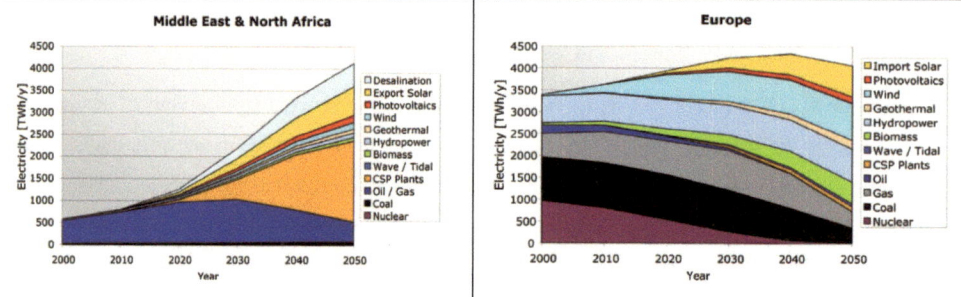

Figure 11: Electricity generated in MENA and Europe
Source: Trieb, F./Müller-Steinhagen, H. (2009): The DESERTEC Concept - Sustainable Electricity and Water for Europe, Middle East and North Africa, in: The Club of Rome (ed.): Clean Power from Deserts - The DE-SERTEC Concept for Energy, Water and Climate Security. White Book, 4th edition, Bonn, P. 25 – 46, P. 33.

Figure 12 shows the scenario typology applied to the DESERTEC scenario. Since only one scenario is described (focused scenario) and an examination of only a small amount of driving forces the scenario is neglecting the uncertainty in the energy system. Furthermore the lack of a narrative storyline from the present to future leads to a classification to a situation scenario and low-effort communication, representing deficits in the scenario development process. Since its methodical and analytical deficits, the DESERTEC concept cannot be regarded as a scenario in accordance to the typology. Since its guiding direction to the normative goal of the shift to a renewable energy system it has to be referred as a vision.

Level	Characteristic	Possible Variations		
Purpose	Time Scale	Long Term		Short Term
	Vantage Point	Normative		Explorative
	Subject	Issue	Area	Institution
	Temporal Nature	Process		Situation
	Spatial Scale	Global/Supranational		National/Regional

---

[87]Trieb, F./Müller-Steinhagen, H. (2009): The DESERTEC Concept - Sustainable Electricity and Water for Europe, Middle East and North Africa, in: The Club of Rome (ed.): Clean Power from Deserts - The DE-SERTEC Concept for Energy, Water and Climate Security. White Book, 4th Edition, Bonn, P. 25–46, P. 25-44.

System	Data Collection	Desk Research		Participatory Approach
Analysis	Nature of Data	Qualitative	Quantitative	Both types
Modelling	Driving Forces	Small (>10)	Medium (10-20)	Large (<20)
	Nature of Dynamics	Peripheral		Trend
Selecting	Scenario Building	Inductive	Deductive	Incremental
	Deviation	Focused	Planning Focused	Alternative
	Probability Estimation	Prognosis		Projection
Comm.	Effort	Low	Medium	High
Application	Preciseness of Problem	Decision		Orientation
	Manoeuvrability	Environmental	Area of Influence	System Scenario

Figure 12: DESERTEC Typology
Source: Own Illustration

2.4.2 EU-Roadmap 2050

Based on the goal of the reduction of European greenhouse gases by 80% below 1990 level until 2050 the European Union assessed with the EU-Roadmap 2050 possible scenarios to achieve this target. The various results of the scenarios are compared with a baseline scenario, which has been conducted by the IEA in its 2009 World Energy Outlook.

All of the scenarios are conducted on the basis of commercially available or late-stage development technologies and no fundamental changes in lifestyle of human beings. All scenarios are characterized by energy efficiency improvements of 2% p.a. and replacement of fossil fuels in buildings and vehicles as well as further emission abatement measures as the implementation of CCS in industry and afforestation. Therefore all scenarios assume an utilisation of 200 million electric and fuel cell vehicles as well as 100 million heat pumps. The final electricity demand, based on all electricity efficiency measures together with a growing electricity demand caused by electric cars and heat pumps is assumed to amount for 4.900 TWh/a in the European Union, including Switzerland and Norway.

In all scenarios fundamental changes in the energy system are needed, especially the decarbonisation of the power supply. Three different pathways, with a focus either on renewable, nuclear or carbon capture and storage (CCS) technologies have been examined that result to the desired endstate in 2050. In its renewable pathway scenario the share of renewable energy of the total primary energy demand increases to 80% or even 100% if solar power is imported from MENA. It requires an installation of 5.000 km^2 of solar panels and 100.000 wind turbines as well as a HVDC grid throughout Europe. The nuclear pathway scenario is also characterized by a significant rise in the share of renewable combined with an increase of the nuclear share up to 30 % of the total primary energy demand until 2050. For the realisation of that scenario 100 new nuclear plants, each equipped with Generation III reactor standards have to be built. The CCS pathway scenario is again characterized by a significant raise of renewable energy and a reduction of fossil sources to 30% of the primary energy demand. All the remaining fossil power plants are equipped with CCS technology. A transportation and storage infrastructure is needed to bring the captured CO_2 to its final storage.

The increased required capital needed for generation, transmission and backup capacity amounts 2.750 billion Euro, that will reduce the growth of GDP by 0,02% in the next ten years. In the period from 2020-2050 the cost of energy is already cheaper than in the baseline scenario, leading to an increase of GDP growth that could be even increased if Europe maintains a leading position in clean technologies. The EU-Roadmap concludes that the changes in the energy system require strong policies and regulations from European policymakers in order to mobilize the vast resources.[88]

Figure 13 represents the scenario typology applied to the EU-Roadmap 2050. It has mainly similarities with the DESERTEC vision, but since the inclusion of stakeholders in the scenario development process it is categorized as a participatory approach of data collection. Furthermore the use of a large number of driving forces and the description of three scenarios it is able to cover the uncertainty in the energy system. The scenario shows only one methodical deficit, which is the effort of communication. The narrative storylines are only mentioned implicitly and there is no description of the way the political framework has to change in order to achieve the target of 80% less greenhouse gas emissions.

---

[88]European Union (ed.) (2010): Roadmap 2050 – Practical Guide to a prosperous, low carbon Europe. Full Report, http://www.roadmap2050.eu/downloads, January 16th 2012, P. 6-23.

Level	Characteristic	Possible Variations		
Purpose	*Time Scale*	Long Term	Short Term	
	Vantage Point	Normative	Explorative	
	Subject	Issue	Area	Institution
	Temporal Nature	Process	Situation	
	Spatial Scale	Global/Supranational	National/Regional	
System Analysis	*Data Collection*	Desk Research	Participatory Approach	
	Nature of Data	Qualitative	Quantitative	Both types
Modelling	*Driving Forces*	Small (>10)	Medium (10-20)	Large (<20)
	Nature of Dynamics	Peripheral	Trend	
Selecting	*Scenario Building*	Inductive	Deductive	Incremental
	Deviation	Focused	Planning Focused	Alternative
	Probability Estimation	Prognosis	Projection	
Comm.	*Effort*	Low	Medium	High
Application	*Preciseness of Problem*	Decision	Orientation	
	Manoeuvrability	Environmental	Area of Influence	System Scenario

Figure 13: The EU-Roadmap 2050 typology
Source: Own Illustration

2.4.3 Greenpeace [R]evolution

The Energy [R]evolution scenarios were produced by Greenpeace International and the European Renewable Energy Council. They are blueprints for the reduction of CO_2 emissions to avoid devastating damages caused by climate change, whereas securing worldwide energy supply and economic development. Other than all the other analyzed studies it has next to the goal of achieving a maximum temperature increase of 2°C, also the second goal to supply all human beings with affordable energy supply.

The report describes three possible scenarios up to the year 2050: a Reference scenario, an Energy [R]evolution scenario and an advanced Energy [R]evolution scenario. The Reference scenario has been conducted by the International Energy Agency (IEA) in its 2009 World Energy Outlook. It assumes an average worldwide GDP growth of 3,1% until 2030, with China and India being the fastest growing regions. The final energy consumption is assumed to rise from the current 66,935 PJ/a in 2007 to 72,483 PJ/a in the year 2050.

Based on the Reference scenario the two Energy [R]evolution scenarios are examining what changes are needed until 2050 to achieve the target of a reduction of energy related CO_2 emissions by 50% in the Energy [R]evolution scenario and 82% in the advanced version from their 1990 levels. The differences between the Energy [R]evolution and its advanced version is due the fact that in the second it is assumed that coal-fired power plants have shorter technical lifetimes of 20 years instead of 40 years. To achieve these goals both scenarios are characterized by significant increases in energy efficiency leading to a reduced primary energy demand of 46,897 PJ/a in 2050. The transportation sector is characterized by a shift from the road to the rail and an increased use of electric vehicles, where the final energy share of electric vehicles on the road increases to 8.6% in 2020 and to over 91% by 2050.

As shown in Figure 14, the energy mix in the two [E]energy Revolution scenarios is characterized by a strong increase of renewable energy sources, especially after 2020 with geothermal and solar electricity sources rising strongest, both in relative and absolute terms.

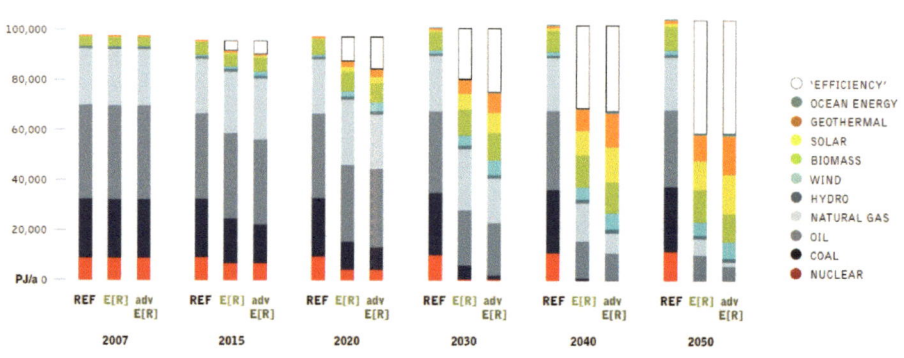

Figure 14: Development of Primary Energy Demand in Energy [R]evolution Scenario
Source: Teske S. *et al.* (2010): Energy [R]evolution. A SUSTAINABLE WORLD ENERGY OUTLOOK, http://www.greenpeace.org/usa/en/media-center/reports/greenpeace-energy-r-evolution/, January 20th 2012, P. 8-14.

To turn the scenarios into reality infrastructure such as district heating systems, smartgrids at decentralized levels as well as HVDC grids on large levels are needed. The additional costs for electricity supply under the advanced Energy [R]evolution scenario will amount to a maximum of $42 billion/a in 2030 and are decreasing thereafter. By 2050 the annual costs of electricity supply will be $183 billion/a below those in the Reference scenario. To support the financing of investment in developing countries successful international climate negotiations are needed that lead in funding mechanisms as the Greenhouse Development Rights (GDR). This Framework developed by EcoEquity and the Stockholm Environment Institute calculates national shares of global greenhouse gas obligations based on a "responsibility and capacity-indicator", showing the countries' contribution to climate change and the ability to pay for investments. Following that principle the USA, accounting for 36.8% of the world's responsibility for climate change, will in turn be responsible for funding 36.3% of the required global emissions reductions.[89]

As the previous two scenarios the Energy [R]evolution is characterized by an inclusion of norms and values and backcasting. The most important methodical difference is that an incremental modeling approach was used, starting from an official future that has been conducted by a third party and using a sensitivity analysis of the driving forces that result in desired end-states. The high uncertainty of the energy system is covered by the use of three scenarios and the examinations of a large amount of driving forces. Furthermore it is characterized by high effort communication since it is representing explicit narrative storylines as well as the needed political changes to achieve the goal.

Level	Characteristic	Possible Variations		
Purpose	Time Scale	Long Term	Short Term	
	Vantage Point	Normative	Explorative	
	Subject	Issue	Area	Institution
	Temporal Nature	Process	Situation	
	Spatial Scale	Global/Supranational	National/Regional	
System Analysis	Data Collection	Desk Research	Participatory Approach	
	Nature of Data	Qualitative	Quantitative	Both types
Modelling	Driving Forces	Small (>10)	Medium (10-20)	Large (<20)
	Nature of Dynamics	Peripheral	Trend	
Selecting	Scenario Building	Inductive	Deductive	Incremental

[89]Cf. Teske S. *et al.* (2010): Energy [R]evolution. A Sustainable World Energy Outlook, http://www.greenpeace.org/usa/en/media-center/reports/greenpeace-energy-r-evolution/, January 20th 2012, P. 8-14.

	Deviation	Focused	Planning Focused	Alternative
	Probability Estimation	Prognosis		Projection
Comm.	*Effort*	Low	Medium	High
Application	*Preciseness of Problem*	Decision		Orientation
	Manoeuvrability	Environmental	Area of Influence	System Scenario

Figure 15: The Energy [R]evolution typology
Source: Own Illustration

2.4.4 World Energy Outlook 2011

The World Energy Outlook is an annual publication by the intergovernmental institution International Energy Agency (IEA) in which several scenarios about the future of the energy system are described.

The energy-related growth of world primary demand for energy is mainly determined by emerging economies, which are responsible of 90% of the projected growth, with China being the energy-hungriest country. The global energy demand is growing by 40% until 2035 reaching about 26.774 PJ/a.

In its latest version in the year 2011 the IEA distinguishes between three scenarios. The central scenario is called New Policies assuming cautious implementation of policy commitments as the reduction of greenhouse gases and the phasing out of fossil subsidies. The share of fossil fuels in global primary consumption decreases slightly to 75% in 2035, whereas the total consumption of fossil energy is increasing. Nuclear power generation is growing significantly by about 70%, led by China, Korea and India. Renewable energy is accounting for half of the new capacity installed and is growing fastest in relative terms. However until 2035 the total supply of all renewable energy sources is still lower than any single fossil source. The energy-related emissions of CO_2 are increasing by 20% to 36,4 Gt in 2035 which is consistent with an global temperature increase in excess of 3,5°C.

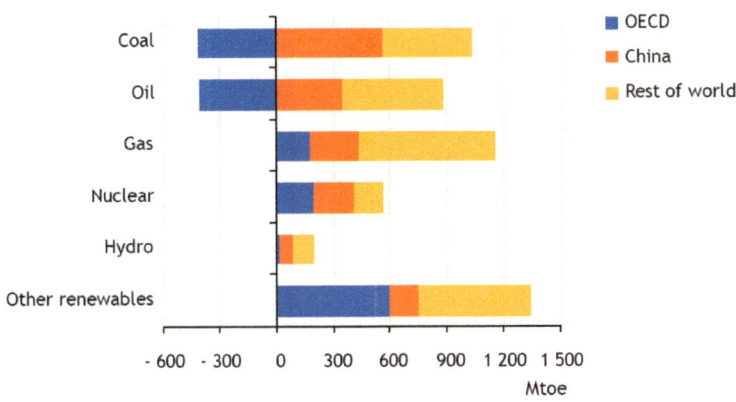

Figure 16: Changes in primary energy demand in New Policy Scenario
Source: Birol F. et.al (2011): World Energy Outlook 2011 Factsheets, http://www.worldenergyoutlook.org/, January 24th 2012, P.1.

The second scenario is scenario is called 450, referring to the amount of 450 ppm CO_2 equivalents in the atmosphere which is consistent with an increase of global temperature of 2°C. Strong political actions are assumed that lead to a 50% possibility of limiting the temperature increase within the 2°C limit. Therefore the primary energy demand is characterized by the lower level of 62% of fossil sources in 2035, with natural gas being the only fossil sources that is growing significantly. CCS is applied in large scales, reducing the greenhouse gases by 18%. In order to achieve the needed significant increase in renewable sources coordinated actions is needed to replace fossil power stations, even before the end of their economic lifetime, as well as the phasing out of subsidies for fossil power generation. The third scenario is called Current Policy and is representing an outlook, in which no changes in policies beyond those already adopted are assumed. The scenario is characterized by a strong use of coal, with a rising demand is by nearly 66% until 2035. Since the absence of clean coal technologies and carbon capture and storage this scenario is leading to an irrepressible climate change.[90]

Figure 17 represents the scenario typology applied to the World Energy Outlook 2011 scenarios. The biggest difference to the previous scenarios is that it is using two explorative scenarios (Current and New Policies), which are taking the present as its starting points. The 450

[90]Birol F. et.al (2011): World Energy Outlook 2011 Factsheets, http://www.worldenergyoutlook.org/, January 24th 2012, P.1-6.

scenario on the other hand is normative and characterized by backcasting, making a 50% possibility for the reaching of the 2°C temperature increase as its desired future. Furthermore it is showing alternative future outcomes, instead of describing in a planning-focused way possible pathways to a sustainable future. Additionally it is able to cover the uncertainty of the energy system and is characterized by a high level of communication, including narrative storylines and needed political changes. To sum it up there are no methodical or analytical deficits in accordance to the scenario typology.

Level	Characteristic	Possible Variations		
Purpose	Time Scale	Long Term		Short Term
	Vantage Point	Normative		Explorative
	Subject	Issue	Area	Institution
	Temporal Nature	Process		Situation
	Spatial Scale	Global/Supranational		National/Regional
System Analysis	Data Collection	Desk Research		Participatory Approach
	Nature of Data	Qualitative	Quantitative	Both types
Modelling	Driving Forces	Small (>10)	Medium (10-20)	Large (<20)
	Nature of Dynamics	Peripheral		Trend
Selecting	Scenario Building	Inductive	Deductive	Incremental
	Deviation	Focused	Planning Focused	Alternative
	Probability Estimation	Prognosis		Projection
Comm.	Effort	Low	Medium	High
Application	Preciseness of Problem	Decision		Orientation
	Manoeuvrability	Environmental	Area of Influence	System Scenario

Figure 17: The World Energy Outlook typology
Source: Own Illustration

2.4.5 Shell Energy Scenarios

The Shell Energy Scenarios are conducted by the company Royal Dutch Shell, which has its business field vertically structured in every field of the oil and gas business, including exploration, production, refining, distribution, petrochemicals, power generation and trading. Next to the fossil energies, the company is also active in the field of renewable energies, as biofuels and hydrogen.

34

In the scenarios the world population is assumed to increase by 40% until 2050 to more than 9 billion people, with the biggest increases in non-OECD countries as China and India. Also a long lasting strong GDP growth is expected in these countries. The total primary energy is assumed to raise from 417 EJ/a in 2000 depending on the scenario to 769 EJ/a or even 880 EJ/a.

There are two different energy scenarios distinguished. Firstly the Scramble scenario, reflecting an inward looking focus of policymakers, who aim to secure energy supply in the near future only for their own countries or supranational entities, in which their countries participate. The attention is on supply-side management of the energy sources, leading to bilateral agreements and local energy resource development. Demand-side management as increased energy efficiency is pushed into the future and only pursued in a meaningful way when supply limitations are accurate or major climate events occur. The atmospheric concentration of CO2 exceeds 550 ppm, leading to a state where a fundamental proportion of economic activity is directed towards the anticipation for the impacts of climate change. As shown in Figure 18 the future energy mix is dependent on the sequential supply responses to the increasing energy demand. Firstly, a strong increase in coal, followed by an increase of biofuels around 2020, followed by a strong increase of renewable then on.

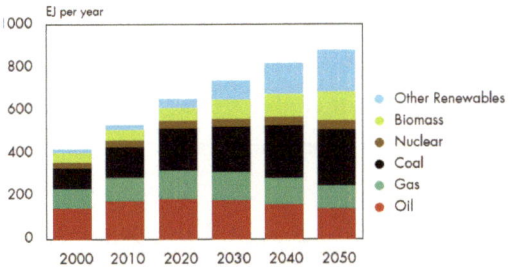

Figure 18: Primary energy by source in Scramble scenario
Source: Royal Dutch Shell (ed.) (2008): Shell Energy Scenarios to 2050, www.shell.com/scenarios, February 10th 2012, P. 17.

The second scenario is called Blueprints, describing a future energy system in which the different objectives as supply concerns, climate change and business opportunities are brought together in new alliances. The initiatives first start at local scales, which become linked with each other when governments intervene in order to harmonize the different measures. Companies, who are expecting new business opportunities, are lobbying for a regulatory clarity. In this scenario also demand-side management, caused by carbon trading and high CO_2 prices, lead to various energy efficiency measures as strong increases in the share of electrical vehicles. The atmospheric CO_2 concentration is limited to 450ppm, which is in accordance with a 50% possibility of reaching the 2°C temperature increase goal. Caused by CO_2 price stimuli the demand for fossil sources is decreasing slightly and the renewable energy sources are strongly increasing from 2020 on to almost 30% of the primary energy demand.[91]

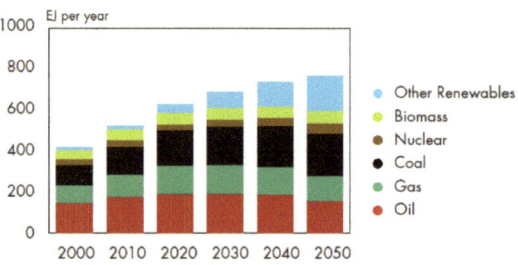

Figure 19: Primary energy by source in Blueprints scenario
Source: Royal Dutch Shell (ed.) (2008): Shell Energy Scenarios to 2050, www.shell.com/scenarios, February 10th 2012, P. 33.

Figure 20 represents the scenario typology applied to the Shell Energy scenarios. The biggest difference is that all the scenarios are not including any norms (explorative scenario) and taking the present as its starting point. Furthermore the scenario is able to cope with the complexity by including several driving forces and the description of more than one scenario. The communication is done on a high-effort level, including tables with the main differences of the scenarios as well as quantifications of main figures. To cut a long matter short the Shell Energy scenarios are characterized by high methodical and analytical quality.

Level	Characteristic	Possible Variations		
	Time Scale	Long Term		Short Term
	Vantage Point	Normative		Explorative
Purpose	Subject	Issue	Area	Institution
	Temporal Nature	Process		Situation
	Spatial Scale	Global/Supranational		National/Regional

[91]Royal Dutch Shell (ed.) (2008): Shell Energy Scenarios to 2050, www.shell.com/scenarios, February 10th 2012, P. 8-41.

System Analysis	*Data Collection*	Desk Research		Participatory Approach
	Nature of Data	Qualitative	Quantitative	Both types
Modelling	*Driving Forces*	Small (>10)	Medium (10-20)	Large (<20)
	Nature of Dynamics	Peripheral		Trend
Selecting	*Scenario Building*	Inductive	Deductive	Incremental
	Deviation	Focused	Planning Focused	Alternative
	Probability Estimation	Prognosis		Projection
Comm.	*Effort*	Low	Medium	High
Application	*Preciseness of Problem*	Decision		Orientation
	Manoeuvrability	Environmental	Area of Influence	System Scenario

Figure 20: The Shell Energy sceneario typology
Source: Own Illustration

3 Conclusion

Because of globalization and other trends as population and GDP growth we are living in a world in which many factors in the external environment are highly uncertain. The use of methods as scenarios that are able to cope with high levels of uncertainty is therefore increasing. The comparison of scenarios reveals that there is broad variety of different methods and approaches used in the development process leading to different forms of scenarios. For a better analysis and comparison of the characteristics and quality of scenarios a typology with 15 variables is developed in this paper.

The application of the typology to scenarios in the energy field is able to show its main analytical and methodical differences, strengths and deficits. The DESERTEC concept, envisioning an energy system with a strong focus on CSP in the Sahara desert, is revealed as not being a scenario, but a vision. The EU-Roadmap 2050, describing pathways to a decarbonised power sector in the European Union is a well worked out scenario, but lacking a high effort in the communication. The Energy [R]evolution scenarios produced by Greenpeace and the World Energy Outlook 2011 scenarios developed by the International Energy Agency are showing no methodical or analytical deficits. Since the World Energy Outlook 2011 scenarios are trying to map all alternative possible futures and the exclusion of norms and values in two scenarios, it is the flagship publication in the field of energy scenarios. The Shell Energy scenarios which are also characterized by high methodical and analytical quality are characterized by the use of an explorative approach leading to future situations, independent of their desirability.

Furthermore the scenarios show that the achievement of a manageable climate change requires fundamental changes in the energy systems. These changes are principally possible, but the political willingness especially on a global level remains the biggest uncertainty. Hence, for the prevention of devastating damages caused by climate change strong political actions are required.

References

Arvidsson N. (2010): Designing More Effective Political Governance of Turbulent Fields: The Case of Health Care, in: Ramírez R. (Ed.)/Selsky, J. (Ed.)/Van der Heijden K. (Ed.): Business Planning for Turbulent Times: New Methods for Applying Scenarios, 2nd ed, London, P.131 -146.

Birol F. *et al.* (2011): World Energy Outlook 2011 Factsheets, http://www.worldenergyoutlook.org/, January 24th 2012.

BP (ed.) (2011): BP Statistical Review of World Energy June 2011, http://bp.com/statisticalreview, October 5th 2011.

Dalkey, N. (1963): An Experimental Application of the Delphi Method to the Use of Experts, in: Management Science, Vol. 9, Issue 4, P. 458-467.

European Union (ed.) (2010): Roadmap 2050 – Practical Guide to a prosperous, low carbon Europe. Full Report, http://www.roadmap2050.eu/downloads, January 16th 2012.

Fink A. (1999): Szenariogestützte Führung industrieller Produktionsunternehmen, Diss., Paderborn.

Forster, P., *et al.* (2007): Changes in Atmospheric Constituents and in Radiative Forcing. in: Solomon, S. *et al.* (eds.): Climate Change 2007: The Physical Science Basis. Contribution of Working Group I to the Fourth Assessment Report of the Intergovernmental Panel on Climate Change, Cambridge and New York, P. 129 -234.

Gobet M./Rubelat F. (1996): The Use and Misuse of Scenarios, in: Long Range Planning, Vol. 29, Issue 2, P. 164-171.

Hartung J./Elpelt B./Klösener K. (2005): Statistik – Lehr und Handbuch der angewandten Statistik, 14.ed., München.

Heugens P./Van Oosterhout J. (2001): To boldly go where no man has gone before: integrating cognitive and physical features in scenario studies, in Futures, Vol. 33, Issue 10, P. 861-872.

Kahn H./Wiener A. (1967): The Year 2000 – A Framework for Speculation on the Next Thirty-Three Years, New York.

Knies, G. (2011): TREC und DESERTEC: Die Entstehung des Konzepts, in: The Club of Rome (ed.): Der DESERTEC Atlas – Weltatlas zu den erneuerbaren Energien, Hamburg, P.114-117.

Lindgren, M./Brandhold, H. (2009): Scenario Planning : The Link between Future and Strategy, rev. and updated ed., Basingstoke.

Masini, E/Vasques J. (2000): Scenarios as Seen from a Human and Social Perspective, in: Technological Forecasting and Social Change, Vol. 5, Issue 1, P. 49-66.

McKibben, B. (2009): Our Energy Challenge – Essay by Bill McKibben, in National Geography, Vol.215, Issue 6, P. 1-96.

Meadows, D. *et al.* (1972): Die Grenzen des Wachstums – Bericht des Club of Rome zur Lage der Menschheit, Stuttgart.

Quaschning V. (2010): Erneuerbare Energien und Klimaschutz – Hintergründe, Techniken, Anlagenplanung, Wirtschaftlichkeit, Munich.

Ramírez R../ Selsky, J./ Van der Heijden K. (2009): Causal Texture Theories of Turbulence & the Growth and Role of Scenario Practices, Working Paper, University of Oxford, Liverpool.

Ramírez R./Selsky, J. /Van der Heijden K. (2010a): Preface, in: Ramírez R. (Ed.)/Selsky, J. (Ed.)/Van der Heijden K. (Ed.): Business Planning for Turbulent Times: New Methods for Applying Scenarios, 2nd ed, London, P. XVI-XX, P.XVI-XVII.

Ramírez R./Selsky, J./Van der Heijden K. (2010b): Conceptual and Historical Overview, in: Ramírez R. (ed.)/Selsky, J. (ed.)/Van der Heijden K. (ed.): Business Planning for Turbulent Times: New Methods for Applying Scenarios, 2nd ed, London, P.17-30.

Ramírez R. (ed.)/Selsky, J. (ed.)/Van der Heijden K. (ed.) (2010c): Business Planning for Turbulent Times: New Methods for Applying Scenarios, 2nd ed, London.

Rao, P. (2000): Sustainable development: Economics and Policy, Malden.

Rogers, P./Jalal, K./Boyd, J. (2008): An Introduction to Sustainable Development, London.

Royal Dutch Shell (ed.) (2008): Shell Energy Scenarios to 2050, www.shell.com/scenarios, February 10th 2012.

Solomon, S. *et al.* (eds.) (2007): Climate Change 2007: The Physical Science Basis. Contribution of Working Group I to the Fourth Assessment Report of the Intergovernmental Panel on Climate Change, Cambridge and New York.

Senge, P. (1992): The Fifth Discipline. The Art & Practice of The Learning Organization, London.

Schnaars, S. (1987): How to Develop and Use Scenarios, in: Long Range Planning, Vol. 20, Issue 1, P. 105-114.

Teske S. *et al.* (2010): Energy [R]evolution. A SUSTAINABLE WORLD ENERGY OUT-LOOK, http://www.greenpeace.org/usa/en/media-center/reports/greenpeace-energy-r-evolution/, January 20th 2012.

The Club of Rome (ed.) (2009): Clean Power from Deserts - The DESERTEC Concept for Energy, Water and Climate Security. White Book, 4th edition, Bonn.

The Club of Rome (ed.) (2011): Der DESERTEC Atlas – Weltatlas zu den erneuerbaren Energien, Hamburg.

Trieb, F. *et al.* (2005): MED-CSP – Concentrating Solar Power for the Mediterranean Region. Final Report, http://www.dlr.de/tt/med-csp, January 12th 2012.

Trieb, F. *et al.* (2006): TRANS-CSP - Trans-Mediterranean Interconnection for Concentrating Solar Power. Final Report, http://www.dlr.de/tt/trans-csp, January 12th 2012.

Trieb, F./Müller-Steinhagen, H. (2009): The DESERTEC Concept - Sustainable Electricity and Water for Europe, Middle East and North Africa, in: The Club of Rome (ed.): Clean Power from Deserts - The DESERTEC Concept for Energy, Water and Climate Security. White Book, 4th edition, Bonn, P. 25 – 46.

Van der Heijden, K. (2010): Scenarios: The Art of Strategic Conversation, 2.ed., Chichester.

Van Notten, P. et al. (2003): An updated scenario typology, in Futures, Vol.35, Issue 5, P. 423-443.

Zürni, S. (2004): Möglichkeiten und Grenzen der Szenarioanalyse – Eine Analyse am Beispiel der Schweizer Energieplanung, Stuttgart and Berlin.